summer sports

© Parramón Ediciones, S.A.
Published by Parramón Ediciones, S.A., Barcelona, Spain
The title of the Spanish edition is *Los deportes en el mar*.
Author: Isidro Sánchez; illustrator: Carme Peris; translated from the
Spanish by Edith Wilson

All inquiries should be addressed to:
Barron's Educational Series, Inc.
250 Wireless Boulevard
Hauppauge, New York 11788

Library of Congress Catalog Card No. 91-35025

International Standard Book No. 0-8120-4865-2

Library of Congress Cataloging-in-Publication Data
Sánchez, Isidro.
    [Deportes en el mar. English]
    Summer sports / Isidro Sánchez, Carme Peris ; [translated from the
Spanish by Edith Wilson].
        p.   cm. — (The World of sports)
    Translation of: Los deportes en el mar.
    Summary: Briefly describes some of the recreational activities enjoyed at
the seashore, such as swimming, waterskiing, surfing, sailing, and fishing.
    ISBN 0-8120-4865-2
    1. Aquatic sports—Juvenile literature.   2. Outdoor recreation—Juvenile
literature.   [1. Aquatic sports.]   I. Peris, Carme, ill.   II. Title.   III. Series:
Sánchez, Isidro. World of sports.
GV770.5.S2613   1992
797—dc20   91-35025
                                                                   CIP
                                                                    AC

Printed in Spain
2345   0987654321

the world of sports

summer sports

Isidro Sánchez

Carme Peris

BARRON'S

We are spending the day at the beach, playing in the sand and swimming. We are also going to try some water sports.

My sister and I are in such a hurry that we take off our T-shirts even before Dad can set up the umbrella.

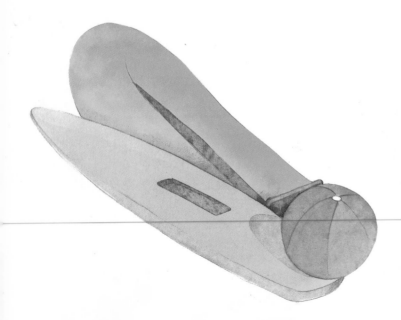

There is room to play all kinds of games on the beach. We can fly a kite, throw a ball, or make castles in the sand with our pails and shovels.

Playing in the water is the most fun of all. We want to show Mom and Dad that we have learned to swim.

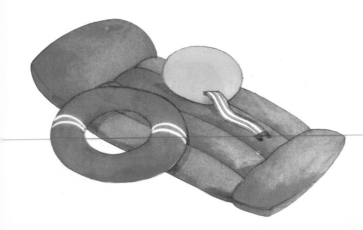

With a snorkeling mask, I can see many amazing things under the sea. I put only my face in the water. The top of the air tube has to stay above the surface so I can breathe.

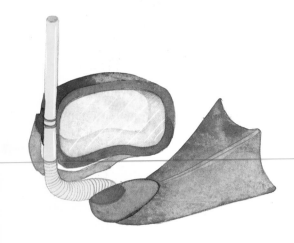

Dad takes us out on a rubber raft. We see some people windsurfing. They stand on their surfboards. Whoosh-sh-sh! The wind and the waves carry them over the water.

Waterskiing is an exciting sport. We watch a skier speed by, skipping and turning on top of the waves. He is pulled by a boat with an outboard motor on the back.

Then we watch a swimming race. The competitors must swim along the whole length of the pier.

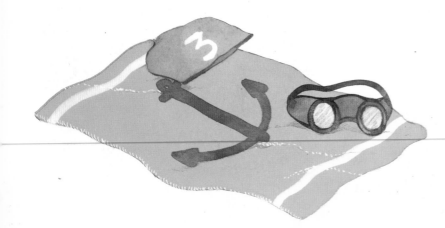

Click, click! Dad takes a picture of the scuba divers as one of them jumps into the water. They look like big frogs in their wet suits, masks, and flippers. They carry tanks of compressed air on their backs.

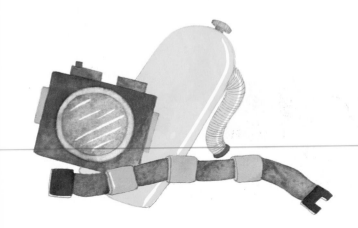

Several sailboats are competing in a race. The crew controls the sails and uses the wind to make the sailboat go fast.

We all take a ride on a big fishing boat.
Several small motorboats go racing by.
They skip over the waves so fast they
almost seem to be flying!

Our new friends show us how they catch fish in a big net. We touch the slippery skin of the shiny fish they have just caught.

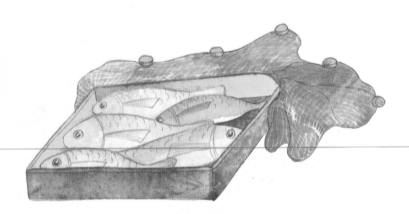

Many people like to fish for the fun of it. Mom lets us try. She shows us how to hold the fishing rod and bait the hook. Maybe we will catch something for our supper!

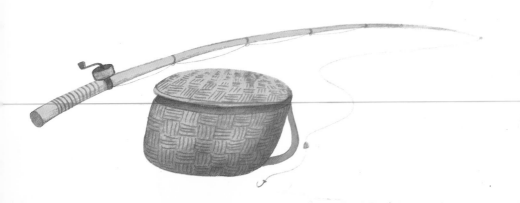

SUMMER SPORTS

Summer Sports

The environment that gives rise to a particular sport determines its characteristics and techniques. That's why many sports are categorized according to their setting or the season of the year: summer sports, winter sports, aerial sports, and so on. The summer sports include marine sports, as well as those practiced in swimming pools, lakes, and rivers; boating, sailing, scuba diving, snorkeling, waterskiing, windsurfing, swimming, water polo, aquatic ballet, rowing, and so on.

Riding the Waves

Surfing originated in the Hawaiian Islands and spread to the West Coast of the United States, Australia, and South Africa. The powerful and towering waves that pound these shores present the ideal conditions for surfing. In recent years, the development of windsurfing has carried this sport to practically all other shores.

The windsurfing board can be constructed of either wood or plastic. The front is rounded and has a small upward curve. It is approximately 6½ feet long and 2 feet wide (2 x .6 m).

The first international competitions were organized in 1966, but windsurfing first became an Olympic sport during the 1984 Games in Los Angeles.

Waterskiing

Water skis are shorter and wider than those used on snow: over 5 feet long and about 6 to 8 inches wide (1.5 m x 15–20 cm). Depending on the event, the skier is towed by a line about 66 feet (20 m) in length and at a speed that varies between 15 and 50 miles (24–80 km) per hour.

The different types of waterskiing competitions are: trick skiing, slalom, jumping, and a combined event.

Trick skiing consists of a series of exercises that are carried out within a course marked out with buoys.

Slalom is done on only one ski. In slalom competition, the skier must maneuver through 6 to 8 gates marked by buoys, which are set out along a course that can be over 1,000 feet (300 m) long.

In ski jumping, the skier must jump a ramp that is 6 feet (1.8 m) high (men's competition) or 5 feet (1.5 m) high (women's competition). The jumpers are scored on distance and form.

The combined competition comprises the points earned in each of the three events already mentioned.

Underwater Sports

Underwater events include both unassisted and scuba (self-contained underwater breathing apparatus) diving. No surface or underwater breathing apparatus is permitted in unassisted diving.

At immersion and during surfacing, the safety of the diver depends on strict adherence to certain decompression techniques consisting of several rest periods at predetermined depths.

Setting Sails to the Wind

To succeed in a regatta event, a competitor must know how to make every square inch of sail count in trapping the slightest breezes. The skipper must also know how to dominate the wind when it is tearing violently at the sails.

Races may be restricted to boats of one type or may allow variations in design and construction. There are rules in the latter type of competition that guarantee an equal chance to win to all participants.

The course and distance of a regatta can take competitors along coastal waters or out to the open ocean.

Sailing has been an Olympic sport since 1900. At the present time, six Olympic classes exist.

Powerboats

Although powerboat competition has many classifications, two of the major divisions are: outboard and inboard. These two groups are further subdivided into several categories—for example, by boat length for outboard boats, and by weight for inboard boats.

Other types of motorboat competition are offshore ocean racing (for large powerboats) and hydroplane racing (for boats that skim over the water). The latter event is probably the most dazzling to the spectator.

Water Activities for the Young Child

Water activities can help a young child gain physical strength and muscular coordination. Swimming and water games can provide the child with:

• new experiences related to moving, hearing, and perceiving space in the water;

• self-confidence that is acquired through domination of the new aquatic environment.

Generally, the child first learns water skills, such as swimming, in a pool. However, the beach can be an invaluable additional resource for helping a young, curious mind discover the rich plant and animal life of sea and shore.

At the beach, a child can also learn about various water sports. The adult can guide a discussion about the characteristics of these sports, the equipment each requires, and so on.

Read and Think Questions for Children

1. Look at the first page of this book. Name some things the family is taking to the beach. What other things might you bring?

2. Why is the father setting up an umbrella? Do you think it is going to rain?

3. Can the children dive all the way under water when they are wearing snorkeling masks? Why or why not?

4. Look at the picture of the scuba divers. Do you know what all their equipment is for?

5. Tell about the different kinds of boats the children saw. Which boat would you most like to ride in? Why?